WHO IS RESPONSIBLE?

SUMMARY

Cat. No: CP32-86/1-2005E

ISBN: 0-660-19532-1

Available through your local bookseller or through
Publishing and Depository Services
Public Works and Government Services Canada
Ottawa, Ontario
KIA OS5

Telephone: (613) 941-5995

Orders only: 1 800 635-7943

Fax: (613) 954-5779 or 1 800 565-7757

Internet: http://publications.gc.ca

CONTENTS

THE COMMISSION OF INQUIRY

Introduction

This Summary provides an overview of the Fact Finding Report of the Commission of Inquiry into the Sponsorship Program and Advertising Activities. It is for information only. The complete Fact Finding Report should be treated as the official version of the Inquiry's report.

Throughout the Fact Finding Report, I have highlighted points indicating findings or conclusions drawn from the evidence. That Report contains a detailed analysis of the underlying events and the reasoning that led me to those conclusions, and in this Summary I will focus primarily on the key findings themselves. The reader is advised to consult the Report in order to understand the context in which I draw any of these conclusions. The Fact Finding Report contains detailed references to source material as endnotes, none of which are found in this Summary.

The Commission's Mandate

I was given a twofold mandate. The first element was "to investigate and report on questions raised, directly or indirectly, by Chapters 3 and 4 of the November 2003 Report of the Auditor General of Canada to the House of Commons with regard to the sponsorship program and advertising activities of the Government of Canada, including:

(i)   the creation of the sponsorship program,

(ii) the selection of communications and advertising agencies,

(iii) the management of the sponsorship program and advertising activities by government officials at all levels,

(iv) the receipt and use of any funds or commissions disbursed in connection with the sponsorship program and advertising activities by any person or organization, and

(v)   any other circumstance directly related to the sponsorship program and advertising activities that the Commissioner considers relevant to fulfilling his mandate..."

The second part of my mandate is to make recommendations, based on my factual findings, to prevent future mismanagement of sponsorship programs or advertising activities. That will be the subject of a second report. It is beyond the Commission's Terms of Reference to express opinions about the appropriateness of the political decisions that preceded the Sponsorship Program.

The Auditor General's November 2003 Report was severely critical of the way that the federal government ran the Sponsorship Program, and that Report comments disapprovingly on certain government management practices in the field of advertising.

The public hearings commenced on September 7, 2004, in Ottawa, and then continued in Montreal until June 17, 2005. Over 136 days of hearings, 172 witnesses were heard.

Ordinarily, Cabinet deliberations are secret and privileged, but the Government agreed to waive this privilege by two Orders in Council which permitted a full inquiry to be made of the question of how certain decisions were reached when the Sponsorship Program was first conceived.

Having studied the many volumes of testimony from those hearings and reviewed a vast quantity of documentary evidence that was put into evidence, I have reached conclusions as to what I consider to be the relevant facts about what happened. On the basis of those facts and my own judgment, I have formed conclusions about and assigned responsibility to various individuals and organizations.

Under the *Inquiries Act*, the Commission was able to carry its investigation beyond the Auditor General's boundaries and outside government administration. I was able to investigate the receipt and use of funds and commissions disbursed in connection with the Sponsorship Program. Through that, I have examined the actions and conduct of communication agencies purportedly acting on behalf of the Government to administer sponsorship projects. I also looked into the commissions and fees those agencies charged, the use of funds derived from the Sponsorship Program, and financial dealings with the Liberal Party of Canada.

The Terms of Reference in paragraph (k) specifically direct me to perform my duties "without expressing any conclusion or recommendation regarding the civil or criminal liability of any person or organization," and I am further instructed by that paragraph "to ensure that the conduct of the Inquiry does not jeopardize any ongoing criminal investigation or criminal proceedings." I was careful to follow those instructions. The reader should not interpret anything said in the Fact Finding Report as an indication that I have come to any conclusions or opinions on the subject of the possible civil or criminal liability of anyone.

The rules of evidence and the procedure followed at a commission of inquiry are very different from those of a court, and the findings of fact that I have reached may not necessarily be the same as those of a court. There are no legal consequences attached to my determinations. My findings are simply findings of fact and statements of opinion which are supported by some evidence in the record of the Inquiry.

I was obliged to resolve many conflicts in the testimony. The Fact Finding Report expresses my conclusions as to which evidence I accept and which I do not. More important, coming to conclusions on the evidence was necessary to fulfill my mandate. The Report would be of little value to Canada's citizens or government if it did not include findings as to the causes of any mismanagement or misconduct that might have occurred. It is equally important to identify persons who, on the basis of the evidence, are innocent of any misconduct or mismanagement.

MAJOR FINDINGS

To understand the evidence presented to the Commission and my analysis of it, the Fact Finding Report must be consulted. It is those facts that allow me to draw the following conclusions:

The Commission of Inquiry Found:

- clear evidence of political involvement in the administration of the Sponsorship Program;

- insufficient oversight at the very senior levels of the public service which allowed program managers to circumvent proper contracting procedures and reporting lines;

- a veil of secrecy surrounding the administration of the Sponsorship Program and an absence of transparency in the contracting process;

- reluctance, for fear of reprisal, by virtually all public servants to go against the will of a manager who was circumventing established policies and who had access to senior political officials;

- gross overcharging by communication agencies for hours worked and goods and services provided;

- inflated commissions, production costs and other expenses charged by communication agencies and their subcontractors, many of which were related businesses;

- the use of the Sponsorship Program for purposes other than national unity or federal visibility because of a lack of objectives, criteria and guidelines for the Program;

- deliberate actions to avoid compliance with federal legislation and policies, including the *Canada Elections Act, Lobbyists Registration Act,* the *Access to Information Act* and *Financial Administration Act,* as well as federal contracting policy and the Treasury Board Transfer Payments Policy;

- a complex web of financial transactions among Public Works and Government Services Canada (PWGSC), Crown Corporations and communication agencies, involving kickbacks and illegal contributions to a political party in the context of the Sponsorship Program;

- five agencies that received large sponsorship contracts regularly channelling money, via legitimate donations or unrecorded cash gifts, to political fundraising activities in Quebec, with the expectation of receiving lucrative government contracts;

- certain agencies carrying on their payrolls individuals who were, in effect, working on Liberal Party matters;

- the existence of a "culture of entitlement" among political officials and bureaucrats involved with the Sponsorship Program, including the receipt of monetary and non-monetary benefits;

- a pattern of activity whereby a public servant in retirement did extensive business with former recipients of Sponsorship Program contracts; and

- the refusal of Ministers, senior officials in the Prime Minister's Office and public servants to acknowledge their responsibility for the problems of mismanagment that occurred.

HISTORY OF THE
SPONSORSHIP PROGRAM

How Did the Sponsorship Program Begin

The "Sponsorship Program" had its origin in 1994-95 when the advertising section of Public Works and Government Services Canada (PWGSC), under its director, Joseph Charles ("Chuck") Guité, disbursed about $2 million from its normal operating budget for what were described as "special programs," at which federal government advertisements were prominently displayed. In 1995-96, nearly $22 million was disbursed by PWGSC for advertising rights at similar events and for expenses related to the promotion of national unity. The objective was to publicize certain federal programs and the federal presence in general.

Following the very close result of the referendum in Quebec on October 30, 1995, the federal Cabinet, at a special meeting held on February 1 and 2, 1996, decided to counteract the sovereignty movement in Quebec by taking steps to make the federal presence more visible across Canada and particularly in Quebec, such as by advertising and displays at community, cultural and sporting events. The advertising group of PWGSC under Mr. Guité was assigned this task. Because Mr. Guité's organization had insufficient in-house expertise, he chose to contract with advertising and communication agencies to manage and administer the sponsorships. In return, these agencies would receive commissions as well as fees paid for "production costs."

The Sponsorship Program was directed in its initial stages, at the request of the Prime Minister, by Jean Pelletier, his Chief of Staff, with the assistance of the Privy Council Office. All of this was done in collaboration with Mr. Guité. When the Honourable Alfonso Gagliano became Minister of PWGSC in June 1997, he took an active role in the direction of the Sponsorship Program, gradually taking over supervision from Mr. Pelletier.

In August 1999, Mr. Guité retired and was replaced as head of the Communication Coordination Services Branch (CCSB), the section within PWGSC that handled sponsorships and advertising, by Pierre Tremblay, formerly Mr. Gagliano's Executive Assistant.

In September 1999, Daniel Leblanc of the *Globe and Mail* made his first request for information about the Sponsorship Program under the *Access to Information Act*. Further requests were being processed during the early months of 2000, and they eventually lead to a series of newspaper articles.

In February 2000, Mr. Gagliano or Deputy Minister Ranald Quail (the question of who made the decision is a matter of controversy) decided to order an internal audit of the Sponsorship Program. The audit report, presented to Mr. Gagliano in September 2000, disclosed a number of irregularities in the administration of the Program. He says that he ordered a temporary suspension of the Program until a plan could be implemented to mitigate the risks identified in the audit. Given that contracts were issued as early as November 2000, the moratorium, if it did occur, was of a very short duration.

On September 1, 2001, after CCSB had been merged with the Canada Information Office, the new organization, Communication Canada, assumed responsibility for the Sponsorship Program. Communication Canada created for the first time an administrative structure for the Program, using known and published criteria and standard procedures.

In January 2002, the Honourable Don Boudria became Minister of PWGSC. The Auditor General advised him in May 2002 that, following an investigation of three sponsorship contracts, the files in question were being referred to the RCMP and there would be a complete audit of the Sponsorship Program from 1997 to 2001. The problems associated with the Program became the subject of daily questions in the House of Commons and extensive critical media coverage.

Since the government's advertising activities were also being administered by CCSB, the Auditor General undertook at the same time to audit the advertising activities of the federal government for the period from November 1997 until 2001. The Auditor General determined that the Sponsorship Program had been the subject of an internal PWGSC audit in 2000 that revealed serious administrative shortcomings. Similar problems had been uncovered in an earlier audit of the government's advertising activities conducted by Ernst & Young in 1996.

On the basis of the initial Report of the Auditor General, on May 23, 2002, Prime Minister Chrétien announced an eight-point plan that included changes to the legislation governing the financing of political parties and candidates for office. On May 26, 2002, the Honourable Ralph Goodale became Minister of PWGSC. He was instructed by Prime Minister Chrétien to "go in there, find out what is the problem and fix it."

Within 24 hours Mr. Goodale determined that the problems with the Program were of such importance that it would be best to again suspend it. The moratorium was partially lifted on July 22, 2002, and when the program was resumed in September of that year, Communication Canada had the responsibility of administering it under new rules and without using the services of communication or advertising agencies as intermediaries.

Conclusions from the Auditor General's Report

The Auditor General's Report is highly critical of the government's handling of the Sponsorship Program and comes to eight principal conclusions:

- Parliament's role was not respected;

- there was a breakdown in internal controls;

- there were problems related to the selection of agencies;

- files were poorly documented;

- amendments were made irregularly;

- there were serious problems relating to section 34 of the *Financial Administration Act*;

- commissions and production costs were excessive; and

- the Government's Transfer Payments Policy was not observed.

In December 2003, when the Right Honourable Paul Martin took office as Prime Minister, the first action taken by the new Cabinet was to cancel the Sponsorship Program. A few months later Communication Canada was dismantled.

From 1994 to 2003, the amount expended by the Government of Canada for special programs and sponsorships totalled $332 million, of which 44.4%, or $147 million, was spent on fees and commissions paid to communication and advertising agencies. These amounts do not include the salaries or costs of the public servants who worked on the Sponsorship Program, the costs of the numerous audits and investigations, or the costs of the present Commission of Inquiry.

Our Inquiry concurs with the conclusions of the Auditor General's Report. In many cases, however, the irregularities and mismanagement that she described were clearly worse and more widespread than she had learned or imagined.

STRUCTURE, RESPONSIBILITY AND LINES OF ACCOUNTABILITY IN THE FEDERAL GOVERNMENT

Roles, Responsibilities, and Accountability of Ministers and Public Servants

The Fact Finding Report describes in detail the structure and lines of accountability in the federal government, including the individual and collective responsibilities of bureaucrats and Ministers. These must be outlined in order to appreciate the absence of oversight and adherence to established procedures.

In brief, **Ministers** are responsible for the departments over which they have overall direction and management. They are accountable to Parliament for how their ministerial responsibilities have been carried out. The Minister must take corrective action should problems occur, correct any problems that have been identified, and accept the consequences if the problem is attributable to the Minister's own actions or inaction. Answerability refers to a duty to inform and explain to Parliament what has occurred in a government department. Ministers are answerable to Parliament for the department under their jurisdiction, even if the questions refer to the administration under a previous Minister. Accordingly, answerability is narrower in scope than accountability.

The **Prime Minister** has special responsibilities in the areas of national unity, national security, and intergovernmental and international affairs. The Right Honourable Jean Chrétien testified that Canadian unity had been his number one priority. There are no established limits to restrict the involvement of the Prime Minister and his senior staff in whatever issue they decide to take over and manage. The Prime Minister's accountability for the government as a whole is heightened by such direct involvement, but in principle individual Ministers retain primary responsibility and accountability for what is done within their portfolios.

The Prime Minister has political staff headed by the Chief of Staff, who generally works more closely than anyone else with the Prime Minister. At least that was the case when Jean Pelletier was Prime Minister Chrétien's Chief of Staff, which covers the period under review by this Commission. Mr. Pelletier was among a select group of advisors and the Prime Minister's closest collaborator.

The **Privy Council Office** (PCO) is responsible for providing the Prime Minister with non-partisan and non-political advice on government policy and operations. The PCO is headed by the Clerk of the Privy Council, who also acts as Secretary to the Cabinet and is the head of the public service. In effect, the Clerk of the Privy Council is the Prime Minister's Deputy Minister, meeting daily with the PM and the Chief of Staff. Jocelyne Bourgon became Clerk on March 28, 1994, until she was succeeded by Mel Cappe on January 18, 1999.

Ministerial responsibility has to do with the relationship between a Minister and the public servants working in the department of which the Minister has charge. Law, tradition or convention dictate that the Minister has sole authority for the management and direction of a department. However, the principle of Cabinet solidarity requires that the Minister seek the approval of or inform other members of the Cabinet regarding policies and decisions that may have relevance to other portfolios and the conduct of government as a whole. In addition, the Minister has an obligation to report to Parliament, which can discharge this obligation only if it is kept informed of the commitment and disbursement of public monies by individual Ministers and their departments.

The size of modern government places a constraint on the attribution of ministerial responsibility. Most commentators say that it is not fair today to hold a Minister responsible for errors or maladministration attributable to departmental officials if the Minister was not aware of them. The exception occurs if it can be determined that the Minister failed to ensure that appropriate systems were in place to manage the risks that led to those errors or mismanagement.

It is incumbent upon a Minister, according to law and the relevant government policies, to work with the public service to assure the proper implementation of government policy delivered through the program or activity under the Minister's charge. Some witnesses, and the submissions made by certain participants, take the position that individual Ministers and Cabinet are limited to formulating policy, and that their administrative officials, directed by the Deputy Minister, are responsible for implementing the policy. Thus, if errors occur in the implementation of policy of which the Minister is unaware, he or she bears no responsibility other than the obligation to take the appropriate corrective measures. According to this view, the Minister is entitled to assume that the public servants charged with the implementation and administration of the policy decisions made by the government will act honestly and competently and will, of their own volition, adopt appropriate practices and procedures in so doing.

Mr. Pelletier testifies that Prime Minister Chrétien, on taking office in 1993, met with all Deputy Ministers and expressed the view that they would be entirely responsible for government administration, and that the politicians would be responsible only for policy decisions. Mr. Pelletier acknowledged that subordinate officials might obtain advice from the Prime Minister's Office (PMO) about a program, such as the Sponsorship Program, while still retaining full responsibility for any administrative decisions, even those following suggestions made by persons such as Mr. Pelletier himself. Mr. Pelletier does not consider this to be political interference in administrative matters.

Ministerial responsibility for a department is to be distinguished from the Minister's responsibility for the **political staff** (also known as **"exempt staff"**) in his or her office. The Minister chooses to employ staff members (they are "exempt" from the general authority of the Public Service Commission, including the appointment process) and works with them closely. A Minister is *personally* responsible for the actions of his or her political staff. Therefore, if a staff member becomes involved in the department's program administration, the Minister is directly and personally responsible for all consequences.

I believe that the proposition that Ministers and their political staff have no responsibility for the proper implementation and administration of government programs and policies is an inadequate and incomplete expression of the principle of ministerial responsibility. The Minister should take steps, in consultation with the Deputy Minister, to see that trained personnel are available to administer any new initiatives and to establish proper procedures and oversight mechanisms. The Minister should give sufficient directions to the Deputy Minister so that the latter will be able to properly supervise the actions of the subordinate personnel. Willful ignorance of administrative inadequacies will not absolve a Minister from responsibility for failures within the department.

The **Deputy Minister** is the principal source of support for a Minister in fulfilling his or her collective and individual responsibilities and, in particular, ensuring sound advice on policy development and implementation, effective departmental management, and the fulfilment of authorities that have been assigned to the Deputy Minister or his officials. The role of a Deputy Minister is to be in charge of program management and departmental administration, but also to be sensitive to the political side. The Minister may exercise some discretion in what is delegated to the Deputy Minister. If there is a disagreement between a Minister and a Deputy Minister, the Minister may contact the Prime Minister, and the Deputy Minister may contact the Clerk of the Privy Council, and the problem would be worked out between them.

Ms. Bourgon agreed that a Deputy Minister would be obliged, in the context of program or project management, to ensure that the appropriate structure, policies, personnel and risk management scheme were in place; that the program or project was within the authority of the department; and that managers had clear delegated authority and information management systems so the Deputy Minister could receive feedback.

The **Treasury Board**, supported by the **Treasury Board Secretariat**, functions as a management board overseeing all federal government operations. Its jurisdiction includes general administrative policy, the organization of the public service, financial management and personnel management. Treasury Board establishes standards through its policies, but it cannot oversee Deputy Ministers' compliance with every transaction. The Treasury Board exercises its oversight role most actively through its review of submissions for spending initiatives. The principal expenditure controls are found in legislation, especially sections 32, 33 and 34 of the *Financial Administration Act*. In brief, section 32 ensures that funds are available to pay for any goods or services contracted; section 33 deals with requisitions for payment; and section 34 ensures that no payment for goods or services requisitioned by the government shall be made unless there is a certification on record that the goods or services have been supplied in accordance with the government contract which authorized the expenditure. These provisions are supplemented by legally binding Treasury Board regulations and non-binding guidelines and policies which public servants must follow.

The **Minister of Finance** establishes the fiscal framework within which overall government spending takes place. Once that framework is set, departments are responsible for the management of the expenditures allocated to them, with general oversight by Treasury Board. The Department of Finance and its Minister have no oversight role for other departments' expenditures, other than setting the financial context via the fiscal framework. The Minister can spend money only after Parliament has approved the spending, and it is primarily the role of that department to ensure proper management and compliance with legislation.

Definition of a "Program"

The Attorney General of Canada argued before the Commission that no Sponsorship Program existed until September 1, 2001, when Communication Canada established formal guidelines, criteria and procedures to govern the administration of sponsorships.

The *Financial Administration Act* and other legislation create responsibilities and obligations where funds are paid out in the context of a program. For example, section 32 of the FAA imposes upon a person "charged with the administration of a program" the duty to "establish procedures and maintain records respecting the control of financial commitments."

The word "program" appears in other sections of the FAA, but it is defined nowhere.

Despite some contrary points of view, I have concluded that the series of projects and initiatives launched by the Government of Canada in 1996 unquestionably constituted a "program." Sponsorship initiatives were a series of projects or activities planned and undertaken to accomplish the objective of enhancing the visibility of the federal presence and promoting its programs and services. As such, they fit precisely into the dictionary definitions of "program." The fact that the program was not formally structured and had not been specifically approved by Cabinet, Treasury Board and the Privy Council Office did not make it less of a program.

Evolution of the Management of Advertising Services within PWGSC

Prior to the election of the Chrétien government in 1993, government advertising was managed by the Advertising Management Group (AMG), an organization within PWGSC directed by Chuck Guité. At some point, AMG changed its name to the Advertising and Public Opinion Research Directorate (APORD) and, a year or two later, it became the Advertising and Public Opinion Research Sector (APORS), always under Mr. Guité's direction.

AMG and APORS were never large organizations. In 1994, the total staff was only 16; only five were involved in advertising—including Mr. Guité as Director, and Andrée LaRose, Huguette Tremblay, Denyse Paquette and Mario Parent. Other employees such as Allan Cutler, Marie Maltais, Evelyn Marcoux, Paul Lauzon and David Myer came and went over the years.

Until November 1994, the contracting function for APORS activities was handled by a separate division of PWGSC known as the Public

Relations and Print Contract Services Sector (PRPCSS). This division led to conflicts between Mr. Guité and PRPCSS.

On November 21, 1994, Mr. Guité wrote a letter to his Assistant Deputy Minister, Richard Neville, about the continuing dispute he was having with PRPCSS as a result of its slowness in completing contracts. His primary recommendation was that clear instructions should be given to PRPCSS that once a requisition had been approved by Mr. Guité's group, PRPCSS was to issue an advertising contract without delay. A second option was to delegate the contracting authority to the client department, subject to prior approval from Mr. Guité's group. The third option, assigning the contracting function to APORS, was chosen, and APORS was given responsibility both for agency selection and for the procurement process, including the signing of contracts. This left Mr. Guité free to ensure that the awarding of advertising contracts would not be subject to a bureaucratic and competitive process. Apparently, from this moment on he felt free to disregard the requirements of Appendix Q to the Treasury Board Contracting Policy which applied to advertising and public opinion procurement.

Mr. Neville testified that he agrees it was not normal that procurement, contracting authority and agency selection would all be performed by the same individuals in the same group. However, he does not recall anyone ever raising this question with the Deputy Minister, Ranald Quail.

Transfer of the contracting function to APORS required Allan Cutler, who had formerly performed this work in PRPCSS, to move to APORS. Mr. Cutler felt that contracting should be done in accordance with Appendix Q, and he was reluctant to perform his functions in the manner that Mr. Guité preferred. When this disagreement resulted in a conflict, Mr. Cutler effectively ceased working within APORS, leaving Mr. Guité free to manage it as he wished.

In July 1995, APORS came under the authority of a different Assistant Deputy Minister, Jim Stobbe. He tended to defer to Mr. Guité's judgment and decisions in advertising matters, requiring only that they be reported to him and the Deputy Minister. These decisions were never questioned, since both Mr. Stobbe and Mr. Quail knew that Mr. Guité was in direct communication with the Prime Minister's Office and, after June 1997, with the Minister of PWGSC, the Honourable Alfonso Gagliano.

After Mr. Gagliano became Minister of PWGSC, Mr. Guité was promoted and given new responsibilities with the creation of CCSB in November 1997. The objective in creating CCSB was to streamline operations, improve delivery of services and eliminate duplication, all with a view to reducing the budget of PWGSC as part of program review. CCSB brought together PRPCSS, APORS and a number of other functions within PWGSC, all under the direction of Mr. Guité. The same small group continued to work on advertising and sponsorships. Mr. Guité made most decisions himself and was not comfortable in delegating authority. There were few administrative procedures, and little structure or organization. The people handling sponsorships contracts all did what Mr. Guité told them to do. There was an atmosphere of secrecy and only the inner circle was informed of decisions.

David Myer was named Director General of Procurement in CCSB in June 1998, but he quickly realized that sponsorship contracts were not given the same treatment as other procurement functions. Effectively, Mr. Myer was excluded from dealing with sponsorship matters except when Mr. Guité was absent and Mr. Myer would sign documents in his place, including certifications for payment.

Financial and Political Context (the Quebec Referendum)

National unity initiatives and what came to be known as the Sponsorship Program were undertaken at a time of severe fiscal restraint. When the Government took power in 1993, one of its highest priorities was to reduce the annual deficit. The reduction and eventual elimination of the deficit were the result of a government-wide exercise known as "program review." Within PWGSC, program review was something of a nightmare to Mr. Quail, who had worked diligently to meet savings targets as a result of the amalgamation of the two departments which formed PWGSC. Program review imposed further reductions— PWGSC personnel were cut by 25%, or about 5,800 people over three years, and its budget was reduced by $350 million out of a total of about $2.2 billion. Mr. Quail was very preoccupied with these adjustments and had little time to deal with problems such as the internal management of APORS.

Program review resulted in the elimination from departmental budgets of reserves of every description, except the Unity Reserve – the principal source of funding in the early years of the Sponsorship Program.

On March 20, 1995, Ms. Bourgon recommended to Mr. Chrétien that he approve the disbursement of $100,000 to two advertising agencies with well-known Liberal affiliations, BCP and Groupe Everest, for the period leading up to the Quebec referendum. There was no prior call for tenders, and they were treated as advertising disbursements by PWGSC.

A Treasury Board submission dated June 15, 1995, requested $20 million to support Canadian Unity initiatives, including $10 million to be disbursed by APORS for advertising, media buys and public opinion research, under PCO's guidance. The Prime Minister signed this submission himself, highlighting the importance he placed on the referendum file. Maintaining Canadian unity was his duty and first priority as Prime Minister. He said that his Cabinet was united in its determination to do whatever was necessary to ensure that winning conditions for sovereignty never arose in Quebec.

After the close result of the 1995 Quebec referendum, the federal government adopted a multifaceted post-referendum strategy. Advertising and sponsorships were only one element. A Cabinet committee chaired by the Honourable Marcel Massé, Minister of Intergovernmental Affairs, recommended at a Cabinet retreat on February 1 and 2, 1996, a "substantial strengthening of the Liberal Party of Quebec," including the hiring of organizers. Most witnesses agreed that such a recommendation would not ordinarily form part of a Cabinet Committee's Report. It is an indication of the failure of some members of the government at that time to consider that any political party other than the Liberal Party of Canada could have a role in promoting federalism in Quebec.

The Commission concludes that a decision in principle was reached at the February 1996 Cabinet retreat to improve federal government advertising and communications to enhance the visibility of the federal presence in Quebec, but that no specific decisions were made by the Ministers present on mechanisms, financing or responsibility for the program. It was left up to the Prime Minister's Office, in consultation with the Privy Council Office, to determine how the decision was to be put into effect. Mr. Chrétien testifies that he decided to designate his Chief of Staff, Jean Pelletier, to be in charge of the National Unity file.

Another result of the Massé Report was the creation of the Canada Information Office (CIO), a new secretariat or agency intended to develop and implement strategy and tactics in terms of communications and policy.

Funding for the Sponsorship Program

Mr. Guité must have learned from someone that APORS would be implementing the government's new visibility program. It is extraordinary that no witness is willing to tell the Commission exactly what transpired in the period following the political decision made by Cabinet on February 1-2, 1996, up to the first meeting between Mr. Guité and Mr. Pelletier on April 16, 1996. It is impossible to believe that there were no meetings or discussions involving the Prime Minister and his staff during that period concerning the implementation of the decision, but Mr. Pelletier purports to have no recollection of what happened. There is no doubt that meetings occurred, during which Mr. Pelletier and to a lesser extent Jean Carle would give Mr. Guité advice in at least some cases with respect to the events that should be sponsored and the amounts to be allowed. Mr. Quail knew that such meetings were taking place.

From 1991 to 1996, a special reserve—the Unity Reserve—was set aside in the Budget for use by the Prime Minister for national unity expenditures. Starting in 1996 or 1997, a specific item of $50 million was included in the Budget to "top up" the Unity Reserve. The funds made available to PWGSC for the Sponsorship Program in its first three years were accessed from the Unity Reserve. In June 1996 the Prime Minister signed a submission to Treasury Board to request an allocation of $17 million to PWGSC for 1997-98. His signature sent a message to everyone about the seriousness of the initiative.

Although then PWGSC Minister Diane Marleau co-signed the Treasury Board submission in 1996, she really knew very little about the reasons why funds were needed or about the subject of sponsorships in general. The list of proposed sponsorships which supported the submission had been discussed with Mr. Pelletier and representatives of PCO, but it was not discussed with her, and she had nothing to do with the administration of the sponsorship contracts that resulted.

At the time, the Program had not been formalized, adequately defined or publicized. Funds were allocated according to discretion given to Mr. Guité, working under the direction of the PMO and with its approval. No directions or guidelines had been given by the PMO or the PCO to anyone as to how the Program was to be administered, what criteria would guide decisions made regarding the use of the funds, how it would be administered and who would supervise implementation of the Program.

On December 18, 1996, in a memorandum to the Prime Minister, Ms. Bourgon expressed concern about ministerial responsibility for funds allocated from the Unity Reserve on the basis of his signature. She was concerned that the Prime Minister had taken on a very large burden of responsibility. She thought that a review of future projects by the PCO or a group of Ministers would provide better management of the $17 million allocated to PWGSC for 1997-98 than was the case in 1996-97.

Mr. Chrétien did not reply in any way to the memorandum. Ms. Bourgon repeated her concerns in a second memorandum dated September 30, 1997, on the subject of access to the Unity Reserve, which was under pressure due to the number of requests for funding that were pending, including requests by PWGSC for an additional $18.8 million for 1997-98, mainly for the Sponsorship Program, and $50 million for each of the following three years.

Ms. Bourgon's second memorandum establishes:

- that the PCO was aware that the PMO was determining those projects to which sponsorship monies were being directed;

- that the Prime Minister was accountable for the use of funds drawn from the Unity Reserve on the basis of his signature on a Treasury Board submission;

- that this accountability could be transferred to a Minister; and

- that, if the Prime Minister preferred to retain accountability, he could obtain advice or assistance from the PCO or a Minister or group of Ministers, who would review projects to be funded by Unity Reserve monies.

Ms. Bourgon attempted to distinguish between responsibility for the nature of the projects envisaged, and responsibility for the particular projects themselves. I was not convinced that such a distinction could be deduced from the text of the memorandum, which is admirably clear.

Mr. Pelletier said Mr. Chrétien fully understood his responsibilities and accountabilities, chose to retain them, and became accountable for how the funds, accessed on his behalf by PWGSC, were spent or misspent.

Mr. Chrétien was also personally responsible for the actions or the inaction of Mr. Pelletier and other exempt staff in his office. He resisted or ignored all suggestions from Ms. Bourgon that sponsorship initiatives and related events would be better directed and controlled by a Minister accustomed to program implementation and familiar with its requirements.

Ms. Marleau and her Deputy Minister had nothing at all to do with managing the Sponsorship Program other than to seek approval for its financing. The Program was run out of the PMO under the direct supervision of Mr. Pelletier, specifically delegated to carry out this responsibility by the Prime Minister. Mr. Pelletier, for all practical purposes, assumed the role, the functions and the responsibilities of a Minister of a department charged with implementing a program. Mr.

Pelletier failed to fulfil that responsibility, in that he did not give adequate direction to the subordinates in PWGSC to whom he was delegating the task of administering a new program. By his conduct and involvement, Mr. Pelletier made it impossible for Ms. Marleau and Mr. Quail to fulfil their responsibilities, since they were excluded from any participation in the decision-making process and had no effective control over the actions of Mr. Guité.

How Were Advertising and Communication Agencies Selected?

Prior to November 1993, the AMG managed by Mr. Guité included two political appointees designated as "consultants." The selection and engagement of advertising agencies to assist the government in its advertising activities were openly done on a political basis. The Cabinet Committee on Communications gave instructions to Mr. Guité on how to proceed. Mr. Guité, at that time a relatively minor public servant, reported directly to Senator Lowell Murray, who presided over the committee. This relationship bypassed the normal chain of command, whereby a public servant is expected to take orders from his or her immediate superior.

Under the Progressive Conservative administration, government departments requiring advertising agencies would inform the AMG, which would hold a competition to choose the agency to be awarded a contract. However, the list of agencies invited to compete was prepared by the political appointees within the AMG. Advertising and communication agencies having Liberal Party sympathies or connections had little or no chance of getting government business. Mr. Guité believes that once the list of candidates had been prepared, the competition was fair, but, of course, only agencies acceptable to the party in power had been put on the list.

During the 1993 election campaign, the Liberal Party promised to spend less government money on advertising and polling and to change selection rules to ensure fair, open and transparent bidding. Once in office, Mr. Chrétien immediately instructed the Treasury Board Secretariat to design and develop a new policy for contracting for communications, opinion research, and advertising services. It later became "Appendix Q" and came into effect on July 6, 1994.

What appears to have been a sincere attempt to depoliticize an openly biased procurement policy was subverted almost from the very beginning. Although early drafts of the proposed guidelines all included price as a relevant selection criterion, Mr. Guité and the advertising industry together mounted a concerted campaign to exclude price. When Appendix Q reached its final form, approved by Treasury Board, all price references had disappeared, although there were references to "value." There must have been a last-minute decision to exclude price. Appendix Q foresees either open bidding for advertising contracts or the creation of a pre-qualified suppliers list by a selection process, followed by competitive bidding for each contract by the agencies listed. Later, sponsorship contracts also were to follow a two-step process, with inclusion of agencies on a pre-qualified suppliers list followed by competitive bidding for each contract.

On February 2, 1995, the requirement in Appendix Q that "only Canadian owned and controlled companies will be considered for advertising contracts" was changed from 51% to 100% ownership. Two advertising agencies, BCP and Vickers & Benson, both close to the Liberal Party, benefited from the new interpretation and became the biggest recipients of advertising contracts reviewed by this Commission. The change took effect on February 2, 1995, the first day of the selection process through which both BCP and Vickers & Benson and three other agencies were selected to provide services for Heritage Canada. This timing cannot be mere coincidence. It would appear that political considerations affected the formulation of an administrative policy.

In practice, the requirements of Appendix Q for a second step, the competitive bidding process, were totally disregarded. In many instances, there were also irregularities in the preparation of the pre-qualified suppliers list. For the next five years, Mr. Guité awarded advertising and sponsorship contracts as he pleased, without respecting the competitive process. No one appears to have questioned the procedures he was following, and no one ever verified whether Mr. Guité and his employees were awarding advertising contracts in accordance with Appendix Q. Indeed, from 1995 on, because of false reports, he was explicitly exempted from making any further reports to Treasury Board.

Use of Communication Agencies for the Sponsorship Program

In the advertising industry, when placing advertisements in various media, the usual practice is to use the services of an Agency of Record (AOR) which, for a fixed commission, verifies that ads have been placed and which pays the various media on the client's behalf. At the outset, the Sponsorship Program did not use an AOR, but on April 1, 1998, a decision was made to use such a mechanism (even though it is not really designed for this purpose).

When a sponsorship contract required creative work such as designing posters, the agency could charge extra for these "production costs," above the set commission fee, based upon various hourly rates for the personnel employed. There was no price competition for production costs; they were usually loosely estimated in advance. Generally, invoices to the government for production costs were almost identical to the amount estimated. No written estimates were requested from the agency, and no records were kept as to the basis upon which PWGSC calculated the estimates.

Following a February 1995 Heritage Canada competition, five of seven communication agencies selected to provide advertising services to Heritage Canada were chosen without competition to supply advertising services to APORS/PWGSC for various sponsorship initiatives. Mr. Guité and Ms. LaRose both acknowledge that the conversion of the Heritage Canada list of pre-qualified suppliers into a list to be used by PWGSC was irregular and did not respect the requirements of Appendix Q. Initially, Lafleur Communication was not put on the pre-qualified suppliers list for either Heritage Canada or PWGSC from the February 1995 competition, yet, between February 9, 1995, and June 30, 1995, this agency received an important number of contracts for advertising services from PWGSC totalling $1,873,998. As a result, the suspicion lingers that the objective of the PWGSC competition held in June 1995 was to qualify Lafleur Communication as quickly as possible in order to remedy the irregularity of granting contracts to an unqualified supplier. This competition was a sham, and the result was most likely pre-determined.

The 1997 competition was not a competition at all. All of the ten agencies making presentations, even those scoring very poorly in comparison to others, became qualified. It may be concluded that Mr. Guité had determined in advance that more assistance from agencies in managing sponsorship contracts was needed, and the fact was overlooked that at least some of the candidates making presentations had relatively poor capabilities. The government policy to ensure that advertising contracts were let through a competitive process was simply disregarded.

ADMINISTRATION OF THE
SPONSORSHIP PROGRAM

Problems of Accountability and Direction

Because Mr. Guité was regularly receiving instructions directly from his Ministers, David Dingwall and Alfonso Gagliano, and because he had direct access to persons in the PMO, including the Chief of Staff of the Prime Minister, Mr. Guité was no longer subject to the authority and direction of his immediate superior, either Richard Neville or James Stobbe, nor was he subject to the authority and oversight of the Deputy Minister, Ranald Quail. In their eyes and those of everyone in the public service, he was in a special category, seemingly exempt from the usual reporting rules, and not obliged to conform to normal practices and procedures. Only one subordinate, Allan Cutler, dared to challenge Mr. Guité's authority and methods and, as a result, he was declared surplus by Mr. Guité. Although Mr. Guité's superiors certainly must have known he had exceeded his authority in the Cutler incident, there was never any reprimand or reproach.

Choice of Events, Amounts and Agencies

Neither Mr. Guité nor the public servants working for him ever received any direction in writing from the PMO, the PCO, his Minister, his Deputy Minister or anyone else on how to select events and amounts for sponsorships. The only guidance was Appendix Q, and it was simply not followed. There was no public announcement of the government's decision to increase its visibility by sponsoring events and activities through PWGSC. We may safely assume that at some point Jean Lafleur had conversations with Mr. Guité during which contracts were discussed and negotiated before they were concluded. It is also apparent that the first list of events to be sponsored, showing the amounts to be paid to the promoter of each of them, was submitted by Mr. Guité to Mr. Pelletier. It is fair to assume that Mr. Guité informed Mr. Pelletier that he was budgeting $17 million for 1996-97 sponsorships, because that amount appears on the draft Treasury Board submission dated April 22, 1996, signed by Ms. Marleau. Because that draft submission included a line for the signature of the Prime Minister, it must have had the approval of Mr. Pelletier, and in order to fix the financial requirements at $17 million, Mr. Guité must have made some sort of a preliminary enumeration of projects and amounts to be allocated.

On May 29, 1996, Éric Lafleur, the vice-president of Lafleur Communication, the agency which handled all sponsorship contracts for PWGSC in 1996-97, sent Ms. LaRose a detailed list of sponsored events that were to be managed by Lafleur, some of which were already the subject of contracts with APORS, although funding had not yet been approved. The list includes details of the commissions and production costs to be paid to the agency, but there is no evidence that this information was communicated to the PMO.

In 1997-98, a second allotment of $17 million from the Unity Reserve was supplemented by additional sums of money from PWGSC's budget or transferred from other budgets. However the evidence remains fragmentary as to how the events found their way initially onto Mr. Guité's list, or how the amount to be allotted to each event was determined.

In the years following, knowledge of the existence of the Sponsorship Program seems to have spread. Certainly there was no shortage of requests for sponsorships. They came directly to Mr. Guité's office or were redirected to APORS from other sources, and an annual master list would be prepared. Mr. Chrétien testifies that it was not necessary to make any public announcement concerning the Program. Yet most of his Ministers testify that they did not become aware of the existence of the Program until it became a subject of public comment and controversy in 2001.

Mr. Guité testifies that he alone made decisions on requests for less than $25,000, but anything larger was decided in consultation with Mr. Pelletier or Mr. Gagliano. The master list would be modified on a number of occasions as the year progressed. Mr. Guité says that periodically he would meet with Mr. Pelletier, sometimes in the presence of Mr. Carle, and they would go over lists of proposed sponsorships, which would be approved after modifications suggested by Mr. Pelletier. Mr. Guité says that he took those suggestions to be instructions.

Since the Commission accepts that Mr. Guité went to his meetings with Mr. Pelletier to obtain advice and suggestions about events and amounts to be paid, it is hardly plausible that he and Mr. Pelletier would have studiously avoided any discussion or mention of the important question of which agency would be hired to manage the event or project on behalf of the Government.

Jacques Corriveau was a former vice-president of the Liberal Party of Canada and a friend of the Prime Minister. In light of Mr. Corriveau's lobbying to persuade PWGSC to sponsor certain events, and his interest that Groupaction Marketing be appointed to manage them, it is unlikely that he would have limited his attempts to influence PWGSC to contacts with Mr. Guité. In turn, Mr. Guité is unequivocal that he was not the decision-maker with respect to Mr. Corriveau's proposals. Mr. Guité produced as evidence a list, in Mr. Pelletier's handwriting, of events and dollar amounts for sponsorships to support his contention that Mr. Pelletier was suggesting events and amounts to him, and was not passively approving Mr. Guité's lists. Mr. Pelletier's version was that he prepared the document as a sort of aide-memoire during a meeting he had with Mr. Guité because the latter had not been taking notes. The proposition that Mr. Pelletier would prepare notes to assist Mr. Guité to remember what had transpired at a meeting is improbable and cannot be reconciled with the rest of Mr. Pelletier's evidence. The list gives credence to Mr. Guité's testimony that Mr. Pelletier was actively promoting certain sponsorships and suggesting the amounts to be paid in at least some cases.

The Commission is of the opinion, in spite of its reservations about the truthfulness of Mr. Guité on other subjects, that his testimony about Mr. Pelletier's role in the choice of events and the amounts to be disbursed to their promoters is credible, whether Mr. Pelletier's suggestions or input were in the form of directions or worded less directly. Suggestions by a person in the position of Mr. Pelletier were the equivalent of an order, and it is probable that Mr. Guité took these suggestions and advice as instructions. I prefer the more logical conclusion that the choice of agencies was a matter in which Mr. Pelletier offered his "input" to Mr. Guité, just as he gave him advice on other aspects of the Sponsorship Program. The choice of agencies was simply too important a decision to leave entirely to a mid-level public servant.

Involvement of Minister Gagliano

The Commission does not accept Mr. Gagliano's testimony that his meetings with Mr. Guité to discuss sponsorships were few and far between, and only of a short duration. Like Mr. Pelletier, Mr. Gagliano testifies that he did no more than give political advice and make suggestions. This statement is not accepted. Mr. Gagliano, like Mr. Pelletier, had the authority to impose his decisions upon Mr. Guité.

Following Mr. Guité's retirement, Pierre Tremblay, his successor and the former Executive Assistant to Minister Gagliano, continued the practice established by Mr. Guité of going to the Minister's office on a regular basis to review lists of proposed sponsorships. Mr. Gagliano delegated more responsibility in this area to his new Executive Assistant, Jean-Marc Bard, with whom Mr. Tremblay met more and more frequently.

The evidence is overwhelming that Mr. Gagliano was a hands-on manager who took a great interest in the Sponsorship Program and an active part in its direction. He is reluctant to accept responsibility for the errors committed in the course of that administration and the political interference which his decision-making constituted. When Mr. Guité says that Mr. Gagliano gave him advice, suggestions and instructions concerning the choice of agencies to handle sponsorship contracts, I am inclined to believe him in spite of Mr. Gagliano's denials.

Reporting Lines and Oversight

When Mr. Stobbe became Mr. Guité's superior, Mr. Quail received a telephone call from Ron Bilodeau at PCO. The clear inference from the call was that Mr. Stobbe's supervision and involvement were not welcome and that people in the PMO preferred him not to interfere. Mr. Stobbe and Mr. Quail understood the message: Mr. Guité's direction of the Sponsorship Program was under the direct supervision of the PMO, and no one should intervene.

Mr. Quail understood that his role in the Sponsorship Program had been reduced to ensuring that Mr. Guité's organization did not spend more money than it had available. As a consequence, the normal authority and oversight of the Deputy Minister virtually ceased. The involvement that the Deputy Minister would normally have in the formulation of a new program, its administration and its oversight did not occur, and his involvement was never sought. With the support and approval of persons at the highest level of the government, Mr. Guité was untouchable and beyond the control of Mr. Quail, in spite of the latter's obligation to manage his department.

Commissions, Fees and Production Costs

The contracts used for sponsorships were the same as those used for the procurement of advertising services. The forms were not well adapted for sponsorships. Personnel at CCSB had only vague ideas as to the services that were to be provided by communication agencies in exchange for their commissions, usually 12 to 15% of the sponsorship's value. No attempt was ever made to negotiate the commission rate downward.

There is no agreement as to what services were to be covered by these commissions and what services deserved additional payment. In the absence of any guidelines on this subject, production costs were established on an ad hoc basis. There are cases where all the hours of a communication agency's employees were billed as a production cost, so that no services at all were provided for the 15% commission.

Examples of Overcharging

The evidence is replete with examples of inflated hourly rates, double billing for services, a failure to seek competing bids for subcontracts, and even invoices for which no services were performed. The full details are found through the later chapters of the Fact Finding Report, which provide a detailed review of five communication agencies in particular. Parallel to the many examples of blantant abuse of public funds is the failure of personnel at PWGSC to challenge or question such excessive charges. This failure cannot be excused.

In some cases, sponsorship contracts were used to purchase tickets to sponsored events. The presence at the Grand Prix in 1998 of the beneficiaries of tickets acquired at the expense of the Government of Canada cannot have contributed in any significant way to the promotion of national unity. The beneficiaries of Mr. Guité's largesse received an advantage or benefit for which the Government received nothing in return.

New Guidelines and Procedures/ Communication Canada

It is reasonable to assume that if the guidelines and procedures introduced in 2001 by Communication Canada to manage the Sponsorship Program had been in place from its inception, the mismanagement and abuses that occurred from 1996 to 2000 would not have been possible. Ralph Goodale, the newly appointed Minister of PWGSC, decided within 24 hours on May 27, 2002, to order a moratorium of the Sponsorship Program to permit him to analyze the situation. He concluded that the contracting out of the administration of a government program of this kind was not appropriate in the circumstances.

The Honourable Lucienne Robillard, President of the Treasury Board, provided the Prime Minister on September 5, 2002 with a series of recommendations for better management, delivery, oversight and transparency. Mr. Chrétien accepted these recommendations and approved the renewal of the Program for one year. The Sponsorship Program was announced publicly for the first time on December 17, 2002. Communication Canada proceeded to manage the Sponsorship Program until it was cancelled in December 2003. Communication Canada was itself disbanded in March 2004.

Earlier Audits and Investigations

There were ongoing indications prior to the Auditor General's Report that things were not right in the administration of sponsorship and advertising contracts within PWGSC. Several previous audits and investigations revealed at least some aspects of the mismanagement.

PWGSC's Audit and Ethics Branch (AEB) conducts periodic audits of its various procurement and program management operations. Such audits are supposed to expose instances of dishonesty, incompetence and error, whether systemic or isolated, so they can be corrected. The Office of the Auditor General is the Government's independent external auditor, reporting directly to Parliament, whereas the AEB reports to the Deputy Minister.

A 1995 analysis of the management control framework in effect at APORS when it first began operations recommended that an audit of compliance with the Contracting Policy be conducted in the future. Even at that early date, Allan Cutler suggested to the auditor that there was bid-rigging and political interference, providing reason enough to call for an audit.

In June 1996 Mr. Guité declared Mr. Cutler's position surplus at a time when Mr. Guité had begun to award sponsorship contracts. It may be presumed that he did not want someone like Mr. Cutler to obstruct or delay his method of handling sponsorship files. After filing a grievance, Mr. Cutler was assigned to a new position and received a letter of apology from an officer of PWGSC, but not from Mr. Guité. The letter acknowledged that senior management of APORS had acted inappropriately and that questionable judgment had been exercised in declaring his position surplus. Mr. Guité was never reproached or reprimanded for his behaviour. If whistleblower legislation is ever to have any teeth, it must protect public servants from this kind of retaliation.

Mr. Cutler's concerns led to the retention of Ernst & Young to conduct an audit in July 1996. The draft report identifies risk areas relating to APORS activities, including: contracts possibly being awarded unfairly and to the benefit of selected contractors; the tendering process possibly being perceived as not transparent and open; and the government not receiving full value for money. These risks do not appear in the final audit report, though it does severely criticize APORS advertising competitions, in which compliance with policy and guidelines was rare. The audit team from Ernst & Young was hard pressed to explain the mild wording of the General Assessment in the Executive Summary. No changes within APORS occurred as a consequence of this audit, and the creation of CCSB did not serve to correct the issues of non-compliance with policies and regulations. It merely concentrated more responsibility and authority in the hands of Mr. Guité, whose improper conduct in disciplining Mr. Cutler had led to the audit in the first place. The audit report was forgotten until 2000, when it was revisited in the context of a new compliance audit.

In 2000, either Mr. Gagliano or the Deputy Minister initiated an internal audit of the Sponsorship Program. It may have been provoked by an access to information (ATI) request on January 11, 2000, by Daniel Leblanc of the *Globe and Mail*. Many of the problems with the administration of the Sponsorship Program described in the 2000 internal audit were similar or identical to the 1996 Ernst & Young findings, and were reinforced again in 2003 by the Auditor General. The 2000 audit made it apparent that CCSB management had not implemented any of the 1996 recommendations. Nevertheless, information was dropped from the final 2000 report, with no mention of the 1996 audit. The reasons given for eliminating all references to the earlier audit are unconvincing. This omission moderated the severity of the criticisms of management and is inconsistent with the obligation of auditors.

A Quick Response Team (QRT) was created in PWGSC in May 2002 to provide answers for anticipated questions in the House of Commons. The QRT systematically reviewed 721 sponsorship files and detailed many of the problems studied by the Auditor General and this Commission.

Kroll Lindquist Avey (which carried out the forensic audit for this Commission) undertook an administrative review of the Sponsorship Program in October 2002 for PWGSC to determine if there should be disciplinary action against employees of PWGSC. It reported on February 4, 2003, that 130 of 136 files had instances of non-compliance with the law or with government policies. The names of the CCSB employees responsible are given in a detailed appendix to the report where Mr. Guité's name is mentioned repeatedly.

Following the Kroll review, PWGSC retained Jacques Demers, Q.C., to head a committee to make recommendations for disciplinary action against those employees who were responsible for non-compliance with Treasury Board policy. This committee produced a detailed report on November 24, 2003. Only minor disciplinary action was taken against two PWGSC employees, neither of whom played an important role in the mismanagement. No manager at PWGSC has suffered any consequence, either financial or to career prospects, because of what occurred in the Sponsorship Program.

Involvement of Crown Corporations and the RCMP

The Auditor General expresses concerns about the involvement of Crown Corporations and the RCMP in the Sponsorship Program. First, transfers of funds from PWGSC to a Crown Corporation or to the RCMP did not conform to the intent of Treasury Board's Policy on Transfer Payments. Any grants or contributions made to a Crown Corporation or agency must have prior Treasury Board approval, or Parliament risks losing control over the appropriations process. Second, Crown Corporations and the RCMP should not receive financial encouragement to promote federal visibility because they are already obliged to do so by virtue of the Treasury Board Federal Identity Program. Third, PWGSC agreed to pay fees and commissions to communication agencies for transferring funds from one department or agency of the Government to another, with little work or services other than the transmission of a cheque. The Commission heard no evidence to contradict the Auditor General's findings. Specific information on various transactions involving Via Rail, Canada Post, the Business Development Bank of Canada, and the RCMP appears in Chapter VIII of the Fact Finding Report.

COMMUNICATION AGENCIES: PRINCIPALS, CONTRACTS AND INTERACTIONS

In the 1995 and 1997 "competitions" conducted under Mr. Guité's management authority, a total of 18 agencies were declared qualified to receive sponsorship contracts, although only five of them (Lafleur, Gosselin, Groupaction, Everest and Coffin) ever actually received a significant number of contracts from PWGSC. Those five agencies were contributors to the Liberal Party of Canada, some with greater enthusiasm and generosity than others. After one of them, the Gosselin agency, became reluctant to make further political contributions, it received a sharply diminished share of sponsorship contracts.

Because of political allegiance and affiliation, the five agencies seemed to be viewed with greater favour in the awarding of sponsorship contracts. Mr. Chrétien declared that "separatist friendly" agencies would not be viewed favourably. An agency could demonstrate that it was "federalist friendly" by making contributions to the party in power. Political contributions were one of the most important reasons agencies were awarded sponsorship contracts, particularly in the opinion of Jean Brault of Groupaction, the most generous contributor.

Jean Brault / Groupaction

Of the executives from the five favoured agencies, Jean Brault gave by far the most comprehensive and candid testimony. The Commission accepts all of Mr. Brault's evidence as credible. If his testimony was on occasion inexact, it was as a result of an involuntary error or a memory lapse. Because of his candour, the Commission was able to examine in detail his contributions to persons acting in various capacities for the Quebec branch of the Liberal Party of Canada (LPCQ).

In particular, Mr. Brault's testimony led the Commission to examine Groupaction's transactions with a group of companies operated by Luc Lemay under the names of Expour and Polygone, which benefited from sponsorships managed by Groupaction and were obtained as a result of representations made by Mr. Corriveau. We believe that Mr. Corriveau's reputation, his friendship with the Prime Minister and his position of influence within the LPCQ were used to further the interests not only of himself but of Mr. Lemay's companies and the LPCQ.

Mr. Brault was encouraged to solicit advertising contracts by Alain Renaud, a businessman who purported to have valuable contacts with key public servants at PWGSC such as Mr. Guité and Andrée LaRose. Mr. Renuad said as well that he had friends at senior levels in the LPCQ and thought he could exploit these contacts to obtain government business for Groupaction. Groupaction informally agreed to reimburse Mr. Renaud for any expenses incurred, with remuneration only for results. Mr. Brault was at the same time making "pitches" to selection committees organized by APORS, resulting in contracts with the CRTC and the Department of Justice.

Mr. Brault acknowledges that Mr. Renaud arranged to introduce him to key players in the LPCQ and in government.They attended the Molson Indy car race in Vancouver in September 1995, where they met Mr. Guité and Mr. Carle. Two weeks earlier, Mr. Brault and Mr. Carle had met in Ottawa, where Groupaction had made a "pitch." Mr. Carle, though initially cold, had seemed to become more receptive to Mr. Brault and told him he should see Mr. Guité and Ms. LaRose. In Vancouver, Mr. Brault learned from Mr. Guité, whom he had also met previously through Mr. Renaud, that APORS administered a substantial budget used for subsidizing events such as the Molson Indy and that communication agencies were engaged to manage such events on behalf of the Government. Mr. Brault understood that this kind of project could be a profitable area of activity for Groupaction. The word "sponsorship" was not yet in use.

On April 16, 1996, Mr. Brault was asked by Mr. Corriveau to engage the services of Serge Gosselin, a person he did not know, and pay him $7,000 per month for a year. Mr. Gosselin may have been working for the LPCQ, under Mr. Corriveau's direction. Mr. Brault agreed to this considerable expense, convinced he would be well compensated by sponsorship contracts. Mr. Gosselin never performed any work for Groupaction or came to its offices. Mr. Brault testifies that the arrangement was confirmed at a dinner meeting on April 25, 1996, attended by Messrs. Corriveau, Benoît Corbeil (Executive Director of the LPCQ), Guité, Gosselin, Renaud and himself. Mr. Guité's presence establishes a direct link between the alleged payments to Mr. Gosselin by Groupaction, to the advantage of the LPCQ, and the public servant responsible for the sponsorship contracts that were later awarded to Groupaction. Mr. Corriveau has no recollection of this dinner meeting or of the arrangement concerning Mr. Gosselin, but Mr. Guité confirms Mr. Brault's testimony, including the presence of Mr. Gosselin. The Commission has no doubt that the dinner occurred, that the persons mentioned by Mr. Brault attended, and that the purpose and results described by Mr. Brault are correct.

Groupaction made unrecorded cash contributions to the LPCQ on at least three occasions. There can be no doubt about the direct relationship between the sums paid by Groupaction to Mr. Renaud's company and the contribution by the latter to the LPCQ. Groupaction made an illegal and unrecorded campaign contribution of $50,000 to the LPCQ by means of false invoices. Mr. Brault received various requests for contributions, and he generally complied.

In September 2000, Groupaction parted ways with Mr. Renaud. Even though Mr. Renaud cashed a $25,000 advance from Groupaction, he went to work for one of its competitors. Legal threats over bonuses were settled for $25,000, paid on false invoices from Communications Art Tellier Inc., which belonged to Mr. Renaud's brother. Mr. Renaud quickly realized he could not earn the same kind of money he had with Groupaction. Within months of Mr. Renaud's leaving the agency, Mr. Brault was being pressured to rehire him. By this time Groupaction had acquired two of the other agencies —Gosselin Communications and Lafleur Communication.

Mr. Brault says that in May 2001, Mr. Renaud called and proposed a dinner meeting where his rehiring by Groupaction was raised repeatedly. Tony Mignacca, a member of Mr. Gagliano's entourage, made a prearranged call to Mr. Renaud during the dinner. He spoke to Mr. Brault, asking whether he would be "looking after" Mr. Renaud. Mr. Mignacca arrived a short time later and pressured Mr. Brault to rehire Mr. Renaud, intimating that Groupaction's contract with Via Rail would otherwise be in jeopardy. Although both Mr. Renaud and Mr. Mignacca deny this meeting, their stories are probably untrue. Indeed, most of Mr. Mignacca's testimony on this issue directly contradicts Mr. Renaud's testimony. There is no doubt that Mr. Brault's testimony is truthful. The meeting demonstrates the influence that Mr. Renaud had acquired within the LPCQ. It is reasonable to deduce that Mr. Mignacca attempted to pressure Mr. Brault because Mr. Gagliano wanted Groupaction to continue to be generous to Mr. Renaud and through him to the LPCQ.

Mr. Renaud arranged for Mr. Brault to meet over dinner with Joseph Morselli, a fundraiser with the LPCQ, who expressed the LPCQ's appreciation for Mr. Renaud's work, for Groupaction's contributions, and a hope that its generosity would continue. Mr. Morselli offered his assistance to Groupaction, stating that he had assumed responsibility for the financing of the LPCQ, replacing Mr. Corriveau. At a later meeting, Mr. Morselli asked Mr. Brault to hire Beryl Wajsman at $10,000 per month to continue his LPCQ fundraising efforts. Mr. Brault refused, but proposed to pay $5,000 monthly in cash, which Mr. Morselli accepted. Mr. Brault says that one week later he met Messrs. Morselli and Wajsman at the same restaurant with $5,000 cash in an envelope, which he left on the table. Mr. Wajsman arrived late, and when Mr. Brault went to the washroom, he noticed on his return that the envelope was gone. Both Mr. Morselli and Mr. Wajsman testify that the meeting took place, but deny that any money was exchanged. They both say that the object of the meeting was to confirm the engagement of Mr. Wajsman by Groupaction. It is most improbable that Groupaction would have been interested in the kind of contacts Mr. Wajsman could offer. Moreover, some aspects of the versions of the meeting given by Messrs. Morselli and Wajsman do not correspond.

Groupaction's unrecorded contributions deserve to be denounced. Mr. Brault sought to purchase political influence to obtain more lucrative sponsorship contracts. These motives were improper. The behaviour of the representatives of the LPCQ was equally improper and blameworthy.

Jacques Corriveau / PluriDesign

Mr. Corriveau owned a graphic design business known as PluriDesign Canada Inc., which was engaged by the LPCQ in the 1997 election campaign in Quebec. It billed more than $900,000 for its work, which made the LPCQ PluriDesign's most important client at that time. When some of PluriDesign's invoices were overdue, Mr. Corriveau was able to meet with Mr. Pelletier and Mr. Gagliano in December 1997 to discuss the problem.

Mr. Corriveau met with various persons at different levels of authority within the government where the initiatives later known as the "Sponsorship Program" were discussed. He was invariably perceived by others as a person of substantial influence within the Liberal Party of Canada. Mr. Guité recalls in 1994 or 1995 being summoned to the office of Mr. Dingwall by the latter's Executive Assistant, Warren Kinsella, to meet a gentleman named Corriveau who was "a very very close friend of the Prime Minister." This message was repeated on other occasions: "look after this guy" and "look after this firm." When Mr. Guité was introduced to Mr. Corriveau in Mr. Dingwall's office, he was in the company of Jean Lafleur, although both Mr. Dingwall and Mr. Kinsella testify that they have never met Mr. Lafleur. Mr. Guité's version is accepted.

Each year Mr. Corriveau would ask Mr. Guité or his successor, Mr. Tremblay, for approval of a "very special list" of eight or nine sponsorships of cultural or artistic events or projects. Groupaction was always designated to manage them, although little management was necessary. No one questioned their eligibility, and they were included in a group of projects known as "Unforeseen Events" which cost between $200,000 and $300,000 per year.

Mr. Corriveau says that his recollection of certain events was affected by anesthesia during November 2004 surgery. The Commission remains sceptical about his explanation. On two occasions he contradicted his earlier testimony, intending to mislead the Commission. He deliberately lied to a journalist, saying he had no involvement in the Sponsorship Program. His testimony frequently conflicts with more credible witnesses. His motivation became apparent as the evidence unfolded: Jacques Corriveau was the central figure in an elaborate kickback scheme by which he enriched himself personally and provided funds and benefits to the LPCQ.

Luc Lemay / Polygone and Expour

Mr. Lemay is a respectable businessman whose enterprises, Polygone and Expour, arranged and managed shows and exhibitions and also published specialized magazines. In 1996 one of Mr. Lemay's employees was Denis Coderre, a personal friend of Mr. Renaud. In August or September 1996, most probably at the initiative of Mr. Coderre, Messrs. Brault and Renaud were invited to meet Mr. Lemay, his associate Michel Bibeau, and Mr. Corriveau, where Mr. Corriveau explained a major exhibition that was planned at the Olympic Stadium in Montreal in 1997 – the Salon National du Grand Air de Montreal. Mr. Lemay says that Mr. Corriveau put him in touch with Claude Boulay of Groupe Everest, which was contracted to handle publicity and public relations for the Salon. Mr. Corriveau denies this, but the Commission prefers Mr. Lemay's recollection.

Polygone and Groupe Everest then entered into a contract in November 1996, by which Polygone gave Everest a three-year exclusive mandate to represent it for a 20% commission on new sponsorships and a 15% commission for renewals. Mr. Lemay says he did not know that the federal government was using sponsorships, and he was thinking only of sponsorships by commercial firms. Mr. Corriveau testifies that his only involvement was design work, for which Polygone agreed to pay $125,000. He says that he was not instrumental in hiring Groupe Everest, but this testimony is difficult to reconcile with documents establishing that PluriDesign also billed Groupe Everest $23,950 plus taxes for professional services relating to the same exhibition.

In January 1997 Mr. Corriveau advised Mr. Lemay that he expected to obtain a "subsidy" from the federal government for the Salon National du Grand Air de Montréal. Mr. Lemay was pleasantly surprised to learn that his company would receive $400,000 from PWGSC. In fact, the subsidy was the result of the first sponsorship contract to Groupe Everest, dated February 3, 1997. Payment was ultimately $450,000. To receive the subsidy, Mr. Lemay was instructed by Mr. Boulay to send Groupe Everest two invoices, for $200,000 and $250,000. Mr. Corriveau acknowledges that he was the person responsible for this windfall, having learned through his government contacts that there was a Sponsorship Program to promote the visibility of the federal government in Quebec. Groupe Everest subsequently managed two other sponsorship contracts for Mr. Lemay.

The April 1996 meeting with Mr. Brault and Mr. Guité to arrange the hiring of Mr. Gosselin must have been one of the sources of Mr. Corriveau's awareness of the Sponsorship Program. He was part of the inner circle of persons connected to the LPCQ who knew about the Sponsorship Program when it still had not been publicized. Mr. Lemay's enterprises offered Mr. Corriveau, an insider, a golden opportunity to cash in on his knowledge of the Program.

From 1998 until the end of the Sponsorship Program, Mr. Corriveau obtained many sponsorships from PWGSC for Expour and Polygone. PluriDesign invoices do not reference a commission of 17.65%, but instead contain descriptions of services allegedly rendered. In almost all cases, the services described were simply not rendered and the invoices were designed to mask the commission agreement, probably to hide the fact that Mr. Corriveau was not registered as a paid lobbyist. Mr. Corriveau states that he was not familiar with the requirements of the law governing lobbyists, a statement that the Commission does not believe, considering his general knowledge and long experience in governmental affairs. Mr. Lemay's companies paid PluriDesign commissions of more than $6 million from 1997 to 2004 for over $41 million worth of sponsorship contracts. All were solicited by Mr. Corriveau, whose chief qualification was his political connections with the Liberal Party of Canada.

Contributions to the Liberal Party of Canada (Quebec)

Mr. Brault says that he was continually asked to make various contributions to the LPCQ over and above the salary and bonuses to Mr. Renaud. To put some order into the cost of doing business, he agreed with Mr. Corriveau that Groupaction would pay PluriDesign 10% of the commission income it was earning as a result of managing the sponsorship contracts awarded to Mr. Lemay's companies. Mr. Lemay was not aware of this arrangement..

Commissions from Groupaction were claimed by way of false and misleading invoices. Mr. Corriveau testifies that Mr. Brault did not wish Mr. Renaud to learn of the commissions paid to PluriDesign for fear that this would enable Mr. Renaud to claim higher commissions or bonuses from Groupaction. Mr. Brault gives an entirely different description of the intention of the parties. He says that the commissions were payable to PluriDesign on the understanding that the amounts would be remitted to the LPCQ. Mr. Brault admits that it was impossible for him to know if, in fact, Mr. Corriveau was sending the amounts thus remitted on to the LPCQ or if he was retaining them for his own benefit.

In 2000, Mr. Corbeil, former Executive Director of the Quebec wing of the Liberal Party of Canada, asked Mr. Brault for a "contribution" of $400,000, later reduced to $200,000. Mr. Corbeil assured Mr. Brault that sponsorship contracts to be awarded to Groupaction in April 2001 would more than compensate him. Mr. Brault testifies he made a further payment of $60,000, although there is no evidence other than his testimony. On this alleged contribution, the testimony is insufficient. It should not be included with others he probably gave to the LPCQ.

There is no documentation indicating that PluriDesign sent Groupaction additional invoices after November 29, 2000. It should be noted that, early in 2001, Mr. Brault met Mr. Morselli, who was now in charge of LPCQ finances, replacing Mr. Corriveau. The meeting explains to my satisfaction why no further amounts were claimed by or paid to PluriDesign. The Commission accepts Mr. Brault's version of the reason for the payment of these commissions and rejects Mr. Corriveau's explanations as untrue.

Mr. Brault says that he found the commissions a heavy financial burden. He asked Mr. Lemay to share some of the load, and Mr. Lemay agreed. Accordingly, Groupaction and some of its affiliates invoiced Expour and Polygone the sum of $2,097,800, from 1997-98 to 2001-02. Mr. Lemay's version of these payments is somewhat different. Mr. Brault told him that he was spending more time than he had originally expected in managing the Polygone and Expour sponsorships and this commitment was reflected in his invoices. I prefer the franker and more believable explanation given by Mr. Brault for the invoices of $2,097,800.

In May 2001 Daniel Dezainde was appointed Executive Director of the LPCQ. He says that Mr. Gagliano told him that if he needed funds, he should notify either Mr. Morselli or the Minister's Executive Assistant, Mr. Bard. Mr. Morselli hired Mr. Wajsman to assist him, and agreed that the LPCQ would pay him a salary of $5,000 per month. Mr. Dezainde, unhappy with Mr. Wajsman's fundraising approach, decided that Mr. Wajsman's contract should be terminated. Mr. Gagliano did not support this decision. Mr. Morselli was more direct, telling Mr. Dezainde they were now at war.

Mr. Dezainde appealed for advice and assistance to Mr. Corriveau, who was not ready to help and said he was unwilling to become involved in any activities other than selling tickets as long as Mr. Morselli was involved in the Party's finances. Mr. Dezainde says he had two more lunches with Mr. Corriveau during the summer of 2001. On the second occasion, Mr. Corriveau made a startling declaration: he had already done enough for the Party and that, in the past, he had organized a kickback scheme on commissions paid to communication agencies, retaining a portion for himself and putting the rest at the LPCQ's disposal. Mr. Corriveau denies this scheme and says he made no statement or admission about a system of kickbacks, either then or at any other time. Mr. Dezainde, however, is an entirely credible witness. Much of his testimony is corroborated and confirmed by Françoise Patry, President of the LPCQ, and he told the authorities about it just before he testified before the Commission.

Mr. Brault's testimony about payments made by Groupaction to PluriDesign, along with the admission made by Mr. Corriveau to Mr. Dezainde, leaves me to conclude that Mr. Corriveau was at the heart of an elaborate kickback scheme, whereby at least some of the sums of money paid by Groupaction to PluriDesign were used by Mr. Corriveau to the advantage of the LPCQ. Mr. Corriveau was paid for his influence in obtaining sponsorship contracts for Mr. Lemay's companies which, at Mr. Corriveau's request, were managed by Groupaction.

One way the sums received from Groupaction were used for the advantage of the LPCQ was by putting LPCQ employees on the PluriDesign payroll. Mr. Corriveau recalls that Mr. Béliveau asked him to look after the salaries of some LPCQ workers, but it was probably Mr. Corbeil who made the request. On this question, Mr. Corriveau's testimony is not credible. Mr. Corriveau acknowledges that when Serge Gosselin was employed and remunerated by PluriDesign, at least 50% of his time was devoted to work for the LPCQ. The financial advantage to the LPCQ was $109,312.27. I am satisfied that there was a relationship between the financial advantage conferred on the LPCQ by PluriDesign and the kickbacks paid from Groupaction.

There is additional evidence that Mr. Corriveau was instrumental in directing cash payments to senior LPCQ officers. The source of the cash cannot be determined, but it is safe to assume that it did not originate from legitimate fundraising activities, but from sums of money paid by communication agencies to Mr. Corriveau or PluriDesign.

Michel Béliveau, in 1996, at the request of Mr. Gagliano, accepted the position of Executive Director of the LPCQ. Through Mr. Renaud, Mr. Béliveau met Jean Brault and became aware of Groupaction's business and its willingness to contribute to the LPCQ. Mr. Béliveau asked Mr. Renaud to solicit various contributions from Groupaction. Despite Mr. Renaud's denial, Mr. Béliveau's testimony is corroborated by Mr. Brault. Different cash contributions were received, in sealed envelopes, to assist in by-elections throughout the province. These envelopes were received by Benoît Corbeil and another LPCQ official, Marc-Yvan Côté.

Mr. Béliveau insisted that he alone bears the responsibility for the irregularities and that his lifelong friend Jean Chrétien knew nothing about these matters. Some aspects of his testimony are incongruous and implausible. I am left with the strong impression that Mr. Béliveau has not told the Commission everything he knows. However, he has clearly established that he could turn to Mr. Corriveau for money, and that the cash came from unrecorded and improper sources. Mr. Corriveau flatly denies that he delivered cash to Mr. Béliveau at any time, but this denial, like Mr. Corbeil's, is not credible. Mr. Corriveau repeated many times that all PluriDesign commissions were declared as revenue and that he never remitted any of this money to the LPCQ. He made much of the fact that banking records corroborate his testimony, but none of his personal banking records could be obtained because they were apparently destroyed by his bank.

Although the Commission lacks direct evidence about the source of the funds delivered by Mr. Corriveau to Mr. Béliveau around May 1997, reasonable inferences may be drawn from established facts which do not support any other logical explanation. In 1996, 1997 and 1998 PluriDesign received very considerable amounts of money from corporations subcontracting to Lafleur Communication such as Publicité Dezert, Yuri Kruk Communication Design (Kruk) and Xylo Concept Graphique Inc. (Xylo). A series of invoices were sent by PluriDesign to Publicité Dezert between September 1, 1996, and May 1, 1997, totalling $452,668. None of the invoices have been found, but their existence is established from their accounting records, and Mr. Corriveau acknowledges that they were sent and paid.

One invoice to Publicité Dezert dated March 2, 1998, for $60,000 plus taxes was for an "annual consultation agreement." An invoice dated October 1, 1996, for $60,000 might be for the same annual retainer. Mr. Corriveau is unable to describe any consultations for which the retainer was paid. Éric Lafleur was questioned about the 1998 payment and the identical expense on October 1, 1996. He cannot recall if the "annual retainer" paid in 1998 was paid in other years as well. He is unable to furnish any details about the very substantial sums paid by Publicité Dezert in 1996, 1997 and 1998, but recalls he agreed to pay

$60,000 as a retainer to Mr. Corriveau's company. Éric Lafleur's testimony, like that of his father, Jean Lafleur, is so full of unanswered questions that the only possible conclusion is that they both decided to say they could not remember relevant facts, to avoid truthful answers.

There is a remarkable similarity among four PluriDesign invoices dated March 2, March 18, March 27 and April 2, 1998. Despite four different events and four slightly varying amounts, the text of the invoices is otherwise identical. Is it by chance or coincidence that the pre-tax amounts of these four invoices add up to $100,000? Xylo also engaged the services of PluriDesign, at the suggestion of Jean Lafleur, for part of the work. Ultimately, PluriDesign's invoices were added to or incorporated into Xylo's invoices to Lafleur, which in turn billed the government. There are many other examples of such invoices and questionable billing practices throughout the Fact Finding Report.

Jean Lafleur / Lafleur Communication

Jean Lafleur was the sole shareholder, director and president of Jean Lafleur Communication Marketing Inc. (Lafleur Communication) and its affiliates. On June 30, 1995, Lafleur Communication was declared qualified to receive advertising contracts from PWGSC. It handled a number of events and projects during 1995-96, such as the Montreal Grand Prix, publicity at home games of the Montreal Expos, and the purchase of a large number of Canadian flags. These were called special programs, not sponsorships. With the birth of the Sponsorship Program in 1996-97, Lafleur Communication received contracts totalling $16,362,872. By 2003, the agency had handled contracts totalling $65,464,314. While paying promoters of various events and projects a little more than $26 million, PWGSC paid Lafleur Communication more than $36.5 million in agency commissions, fees and costs.

I judged Mr. Lafleur to be evasive throughout his testimony. It is impossible to accept that an intelligent businessman would be unable to remember such important facts as discussions or meetings he must have had with Mr. Guité in 1996 prior to the signature of contracts involving the expenditure by PWGSC of more than $16 million. Mr. Lafleur's complete absence of memory on these points contrasts with his testimony that Mr. Guité gave him permission to subcontract without competition. It was obvious that the Commission was hearing a witness who wished to appear slow-witted rather than give truthful answers.

On May 29, 1996, Mr. Lafleur's son Éric sent a fax to Andrée LaRose with a detailed list of the sponsorship contracts which Lafleur Communication was already handling for PWGSC, and very detailed lists of events which it expected to handle in 1996. Jean Lafleur professes to have no recollection of any list or of how it might have come to be prepared. Éric has a better memory, and testifies that the list was prepared following meetings and discussions between Mr. Lafleur and Mr. Guité, and that he sent the list to Ms. LaRose at the request of his father.

Lafleur Communication was a generous and regular contributor to the Liberal Party. Jean Lafleur and Éric made additional gifts, as did some Lafleur employees, who were asked by Jean Lafleur to contribute. Two of them were reimbursed by Lafleur Communication for their contributions.

Because of the important role Mr. Pelletier played in the initiation and management of the Sponsorship Program, both he and Jean Lafleur were questioned about their relationship and asked specific questions about when they met for the first time. Their answers to these questions cannot be reconciled, and it must be concluded that at least one of them has not been truthful.

Mr. Pelletier testifies that the first meeting he had with Mr. Lafleur was when the latter came to the PMO to thank him for hiring his son Éric, who had been engaged by the PMO for a trade mission in January 1998. Hence, his first encounter with Mr. Lafleur, according to Mr. Pelletier's testimony, must have been in or about that month. Mr. Lafleur testifies that he invited Mr. Pelletier in the summer or autumn of 1997 to have the first of several meals they shared over the years. He is specific in testifying that this first meal took place before their meeting in the PMO. He insists that at their meal they did not discuss any details of the Sponsorship Program, but may have discussed it in general. Later, he testifies that he does not remember discussing the Program with Mr. Pelletier at their meals. Mr. Pelletier also denied having discussed advertising and sponsorships with Mr. Lafleur.

The evidence leaves two possibilities, the first being that the two had no meal together in 1997. I am not prepared to give serious consideration to this possibility. This leaves the intriguing question of why Mr. Pelletier would prefer not to recall a meal with Mr. Lafleur. The second possibility is that they met for a meal and discussed the Sponsorship Program in general terms. Mr. Pelletier describes himself as an exceedingly busy man. It is highly improbable that in the summer or fall of 1997 he had time for meals with a stranger just for pleasant conversation. It is even more improbable that they would not have talked about the Sponsorship Program, since it had suddenly become the most important source of business for Mr. Lafleur's agency.

The testimony of Mr. Lafleur must also be considered in the light of a memorandum he sent to Mr. Pelletier on June 11, 1998. Mr. Pelletier testifies that prior to that date, the two men met by chance on an Ottawa street, and Mr. Lafleur complained that his volume of sponsorship contracts had diminished sharply. He asked Mr. Pelletier to intervene, and Mr. Pelletier suggested that Mr. Lafleur send him written details of the problem. The memorandum includes a very detailed list of the

$12 million of sponsorship contracts to Lafleur Communication in 1997-98, and the contracts awarded in 1998-99 of only $2,532,200. Added to the lists of past and current contracts are other proposed projects and events.

Nothing resulted from this communication. However, the fact that it was sent establishes that, in the opinion of Mr. Lafleur, Mr. Pelletier was a central figure making decisions about which events to sponsor, and that he was a good person to speak to on the question of which agency would receive sponsorship contracts. Mr. Lafleur did not direct his plea to Mr. Guité or Mr. Gagliano. It is fair to conclude that he had formed his opinion on the basis of his past contacts with Mr. Pelletier, which were, according to both men, limited to their lunches. From all of this, the conclusion is inescapable that, during lunches, they discussed the Sponsorship Program.

There were repeated instances of irregularities and overcharging in the administration of different sponsorship contracts handled by Lafleur Communication, yet no invoice was ever challenged or questioned by the personnel at PWGSC. The most flagrant examples include: production costs and fees for nothing more than opening a file; mock-ups billed at a flat rate of $2,750 each; unjustifiably high hourly rates for the services provided; and inflated hours spent on a project.

The cooperation between Messrs. Lafleur and Guité in justifying the use of subcontractors to get around the intent of the government's contracting policy cannot be excused. The Commission heard no evidence that PWGSC saved any money or time, or gained any expertise, when Lafleur Communication subcontracted sponsorship work to Publicité Dezert. The transparent purpose of the subcontract was twofold: it permitted Publicité Dezert to charge Lafleur Communication a markup on the price it paid to obtain the goods or services it procured from others, and it permitted Lafleur Communication to charge a commission of 17.65% on the amount of the Publicité Dezert invoice. These two surcharges were in addition to the cost to PWGSC of having the subcontract given to a related company without competitive bidding.

The Fact Finding Report illustrates other examples of invoice irregularities involving Lafleur Communication.

Gilles-André Gosselin / Gosselin Communications

Another major recipient of PWGSC sponsorship contracts was Gosselin Communications, owned by Gilles-André Gosselin, a former colleague of Mr. Guité in the Department of Supply and Services. Mr. Gosselin's first Sponsorship Program work was in 1996 as a subcontractor to the Lafleur agency, for the summer 1997 trip of the Bluenose II. Mr. Guité "suggested" to Jean Lafleur that he use Mr.Gosselin's agency, which had not yet qualified to handle PWGSC contracts directly. In fiscal year 1996-97, the Lafleur agency billed PWGSC $255,657.50 for work performed by the Gosselin agency covering 3,549 hours.

Mr. Gosselin had been advised by someone, almost surely his friend Mr. Guité, to move to Ottawa and that, as soon as his agency was qualified to contract with PWGSC, it would be awarded two sponsorship contracts. He was reluctant at first to admit that any contracts had been promised to him in advance, because he obviously knew the discussions were inappropriate. Mr. Guité also refuses to admit to the discussions, including promises he made.

By 1997-98 Gosselin Communications had received sponsorship contracts totalling $7,066,293. The next fiscal year, prior to its October 1998 sale, Gosselin Communications received $14,094,976 in sponsorship contracts. Although there were many instances of improper invoicing, Mr. Gosselin made an effort to fulfil his agency's sponsorship contracts in a more systematic manner than the Lafleur agency. Nevertheless, the Commission saw evidence that the agency regularly billed PWGSC for hours which had not been worked. There is no evidence that PWGSC ever questioned the Gosselin invoices or required validation of the hours of work that were charged.

There is no evidence that political considerations influenced the awarding of sponsorship contracts to Gosselin Communications. When the Gosselin agency was awarded the 1994 and 1995 contracts, the relationship between Mr. Guité, Mr. Gosselin and their wives had evolved into a warm friendship. It is safe to conclude that friendship was at least one of the reasons for the sudden prosperity of Gosselin Communications and the Gosselin family starting in 1997.

Once Mr. Guité had left CCSB, Mr. Gosselin met with Jean-Marc Bard, Mr. Gagliano's Executive Assistant, to discuss the drop in the volume of business to the Gosselin agency. Mr. Bard attributed this to the machinations of Mr. Gosselin's adversaries. Mr. Bard did not protest that he had nothing to do with the allocation of sponsorship contracts, or any ignorance of the factors that led to one agency receiving contracts over another. One may conclude that the factors were known by Mr. Bard to be mainly political.

As of October 1, 1998, Gosselin Communications sold all of its business and assets to a newly created corporation controlled by Jean Brault. Between April 28, 1997, and October 1, 1998, Gosselin Communications handled over $21 million of sponsorship contracts, earning $1.4 million in agency commissions and $8.2 million in production costs. It was also awarded two advertising contracts with a value of $1.5 million. This enabled it to pay salaries and bonuses in excess of $3.3 million to Mr. Gosselin and his wife and his son.

Paul Coffin / Communication Coffin

In 1992 Paul Coffin incorporated Communication Coffin (the Coffin agency) a small operation with only two full-time employees. The Coffin agency qualified to manage advertising and sponsorship contracts on behalf of PWGSC in the selection process on April 28, 1997. In the questionnaire submitted to the selection committee, Mr. Coffin made a number of deliberately false statements about the size of his agency, the number of employees, and the revenues earned in previous years. Mr. Guité probably already knew about the small size of Mr. Coffin's agency from their social and business contacts. The Coffin agency was already working as a subcontractor on a sponsorship contract given to the Lafleur agency. On the date it qualified, it was awarded five sponsorship contracts having a total value of $665,000.

Mr. Coffin and Mr. Guité were good friends, which is almost surely why the Coffin agency handled sponsorship and advertising contracts, since it had no particular qualifications to justify its selection. After Mr. Guité left the public service, Mr. Coffin continued to be awarded contracts by Pierre Tremblay. The Coffin agency looked after sponsorship contracts of more than $8.5 million from 1997 to 2003. Most remarkable is the amount of production costs and fees foreseen, charged and allowed. The promoters of events and projects received $5,392,500 as sponsorships; the Coffin agency received, in commissions, fees and costs a total of over $3 million. In 1998-99 and 1999-2000, revenues earned by the Coffin agency were almost exactly equivalent to the amounts paid to the events being sponsored.

Mr. Coffin admitted the falsification of its accounting records and invoices. He was, when he testified, about to go to trial on eighteen criminal charges of fraud relating to invoices to PWGSC. He pleaded guilty to the charges and submitted an agreed statement of facts preparatory to sentencing submissions.

Claude Boulay / Groupe Everest

Claude Boulay began operating Groupe Everest in 1982. Other partners joined the firm but Mr. Boulay continued to be its president and principal shareholder. In 1996, Mr. Boulay's wife, Diane Deslauriers, started to carry on business with and for Groupe Everest through her personal corporation Caliméro Partenariat Inc. Groupe Everest qualified in February 1995 to receive advertising contracts from Heritage Canada. It immediately began to receive sponsorship contracts from PWGSC once Mr. Guité "extended" the Heritage Canada list of qualified suppliers to cover suppliers to PWGSC.

On October 29, 1997, PWGSC announced a competition to select a new Agency of Record (AOR). Groupe Everest allied itself with two other agencies to form the MediaVision consortium and, on December 15, 1997, was chosen as the new AOR. The contracting party was to be a corporation named Média/IDA Vision Inc., whose obligations would be guaranteed by Groupe Everest. Mr. Boulay must have revealed to Mr. Guité that Média/IDA Vision Inc. was a wholly owned subsidiary of Groupe Everest. MediaVision's presentation to the selection committee had been misleading. It is impossible to know if the selection committee would have made the same choice if it had been aware of the ownership and the true identity of the candidate.

The contract was signed on March 31, 1998, engaging Média/IDA Vision Inc. as the Government's AOR for a five-year period. The net revenues from the operations of Média/IDA Vision Inc. alone between 1998 and 2003 were $1,709,441. After Mr. Goodale's temporary suspension of the Sponsorship Program, the commission payable for media placement was reduced from 17.65% to 11.75%, and the AOR commission was reduced from 3% to 2%. This could have been done years earlier by Mr. Guité or Pierre Tremblay.

Groupe Everest had significant income from its private sector clients, and government sources accounted for only 28% of its total revenues. The Commission saw no evidence of the abusive practices such as billing hours not worked, exaggeration of time charges and overbilling generally in the contracts managed by Groupe Everest. Nevertheless, Mr. Boulay and his associates managed their business in ways which were at best dubious and at worst unethical.

Mr. Boulay and Ms. Deslauriers have been strong supporters of the Liberal Party of Canada. From 1996 to 2003 inclusive, they made political contributions of $194,832 to the Party. Mr. Boulay also worked actively for Paul Martin in 1991, supporting his unsuccessful campaign for the federal Liberal leadership. During the 1993 election campaign they met Mr. Martin frequently. Following the election, Ms. Deslauriers continued to be active in fundraising. Again in 1997, Groupe Everest and Mr. Boulay personally rendered services to the LPCQ in developing and implementing campaign strategy. Although they developed a social friendship with Mr. Martin, there is no evidence that that friendship or their ties to the Liberal Party of Canada were ever invoked by Mr. Boulay in an attempt to influence government officials to direct business or contracts to Groupe Everest, nor is there any credible evidence that Mr. Martin ever had a hand in the awarding of contracts to Mr. Boulay's agency.

Groupe Everest entered into various agreements with its clients to receive a "canvassing commission" paid by the promoter for its efforts in securing the sponsorship from PWGSC, in addition to the usual 12% commission payable by PWGSC to the communication agency managing a sponsorship contract. Double commissions were collected with respect to the sponsorship contracts awarded to Groupe Everest for the Société du Parc des Îles, also with the Jeux de Québec in 2001. In the case of Parc des Îles, the Société received sponsorships for five years starting in 1997, totalling $2,625,000. The usual agency commission of 12% payable by PWGSC to Groupe Everest brought in revenues of $315,000, to which were added production fees of $57,910. Groupe Everest also received commissions from the Societé for the first four years of the sponsorships totalling $343,750. These commissions were not disclosed to PWGSC.

Mr. Boulay and Ms. Deslauriers saw nothing wrong with the practice of collecting a commission from both the promoter of a sponsored event and the client paying the sponsorship money. I believe the loyalty of the communication agency should be to its client, which, in this case, was PWGSC. The public servants in PWGSC are not blameless with respect to the payment of double commissions. Bureaucrats must protect the public purse against any desire for excessive profit of the private sector.

CHUCK GUITÉ AFTER
RETIREMENT/
ORO COMMUNICATIONS

Following Mr. Guité's retirement in 1999, he incorporated Oro Communications. Revenues from consulting fees for fiscal years ending July 31, 2000, 2001 and 2002 totalled $1,039,431. It raises the question of how a former mid-level public servant could command such substantial fees—roughly three times his departing salary.

Several of the persons from communication agencies with whom Mr. Guité, in his capacity as Director of APORS and CCSB, entered into sponsorship and advertising contracts were noticeably reticent about testifying about their conversations and discussions with him in 1996 and 1997. Jean Lafleur professed to have no recollection of the discussions with Mr. Guité that preceded the sponsorship contracts awarded to his agency in 1996, although he acknowledged that there must have been such discussions. Gilles-André Gosselin was so anxious to avoid testifying about his discussions with Mr. Guité prior to being awarded a series of contracts dated April 28, 1997, that he falsely affirmed that his agency was not working on the contracts prior to that date. In fact, no representative of an agency or subcontractor has been prepared to testify in any detail about their first contacts with Mr. Guité, even though it is fair to assume that he must have given the agencies concerned some sort of explanation about how each contract was to be administered, and how the agency was to be remunerated for its work.

Although Mr. Guité's testimony about the frequency and timing of his many meetings with Mr. Corriveau is credible, he was vague about the substance of conversations they had concerning the sponsorship contracts given by PWGSC to Groupaction for sponsorships to Mr. Lemay's enterprises, saying only that these matters were decided upon "upstairs." We do not know from him how much he knew or might have suspected about Mr. Corriveau's kickback scheme.

No one who was questioned on this topic was willing to disclose openly the details of the early discussions between Mr. Guité and the communication agencies which later handled sponsorship and advertising contracts on behalf of PWGSC because some parts of those discussions involve seriously improper conduct by the participants. The Commission notes at once that virtually all of Oro's clients, with the principal exception of the Institute of Canadian Advertising, received direct benefits from sponsorship or advertising contracts, either as sponsorees or as communication and advertising agencies, during Mr. Guité's tenure at PWGSC.

In October 2001, Oro agreed in writing to provide services related to market development in eastern and western Canada to Groupaction for $87,500, although Mr. Brault testifies that the actual services related to ongoing negotiations for the sale or merger of Groupaction. Given the absence of any evidence of tangible results, it is unlikely these very substantial fees were for "consulting."

Oro's largest single client billings, $371,000 for consultation fees plus expenses, were from PacCanUS Inc., a corporation closely related to Vickers & Benson. Vickers & Benson's President, John Hayter, testifies that Oro was retained because of a possible purchase by Havas, a French corporation. Mr. Hayter hoped that Mr. Guité might be able to find a solution to the problem of the 100% Canadian rule if the purchase took place. An agreement dated March 1, 2000 provides for $1,400 per day, plus commission in the event of a sale.

Mr. Guité says that he met with Mr. Gagliano in March 2000 to ensure that the sale to Havas would not bar Vickers & Benson from receiving government contracts. Mr. Guité proposed that the sale be structured so that, nominally, a wholly Canadian-owned corporation would do business with the government. Mr. Guité says that he received a call from Pierre Tremblay shortly after the meeting with Mr. Gagliano, and was told that Mr. Gagliano had spoken to Ministers Martin and Manley and that the volume of government business of the new entity would be maintained.

Mr. Guité says he informed Mr. Hayter of this result, but Mr. Hayter denies both the conversation and that he asked Mr. Guité to obtain such assurances. Vickers & Benson's government business did not decline after its September 14, 2000 sale to Havas. Mr. Guité received a $100,000 commission, evidenced by correspondence that also asks PacCanUS to pay an outstanding balance. The bill was paid, and the payment tends to corroborate Mr. Guité's testimony about why he was hired. The only plausible explanation for the amount of the payments, which greatly exceeded any rational evaluation of the time and services rendered, is the contracts that Vickers & Benson received from PWGSC prior to Mr. Guité's retirement.

If one were to examine Mr. Guité's post-retirement dealings with each of these agencies one at a time, it would be dangerous to draw conclusions of impropriety. However, there is evidence of many transactions, involving several different agencies and proof of payment of substantial sums of money for alleged "consultations" but virtually no proof of the services provided in exchange.

There is no direct evidence that understandings were concluded with these agencies while Mr. Guité was still in the public service, but the reluctance of witnesses to reveal the substance of their conversations with him at the time when the first contracts were being allocated, combined with the evidence of the payments made to Oro after he retired, permits me to draw the reasonable inference that there had been such understandings, and that Mr. Guité relied upon them to persuade people like Messrs. Brault, Hayter, Lafleur, Coffin and Boulay to enrich him, under the guise of consulting services, once he had retired.

ASSIGNING RESPONSIBILITY

The Fact Finding Report is not a judgment, and the conclusions do not establish the legal responsibility, either civil or criminal, of the persons and organizations singled out for critical comment or a finding of misconduct. The paragraphs that follow should not be read in isolation from the overall conclusions of the Fact Finding Report. The fact that only certain persons or organizations are mentioned in Chapter XVI does not absolve the others assigned blame earlier.

I have identified three main factors that caused or contributed to the problems described in the Report of the Auditor General:

- the unprecedented decision to direct the Sponsorship Program from the PMO, bypassing the departmental procedures and controls which the Deputy Minister of PWGSC would normally have been expected to apply and enforce;

- the failure of the Deputy Minister of PWGSC to provide oversight and administrative safeguards against the misuse of public funds; and

- the deliberate lack of transparency on how the Program was initiated, financed and directed.

The Responsibility of Mr. Chrétien and Mr. Pelletier

Mr. Pelletier must have known that such a program of discretionary spending would be open to error and abuse unless provided with rules, guidelines, controls, safeguards and oversight. The opportunities for misappropriation of public funds and personal gain offered by an unstructured program of grants and contributions such as the Sponsorship Program are enormous. The rules and guidelines prescribed by Treasury Board policies and oversight by deputy ministers and their staff ordinarily provide the framework for honest and competent public servants. However, such policies and oversight are also meant to create an obstacle to dishonesty and incompetence. By choosing to give direction to Mr. Guité personally, Mr. Pelletier bypassed the normal methods of administration of government programs, and effectively eliminated the oversight that would have been provided by Mr. Quail and his department.

The notion that Mr. Pelletier and Mr. Gagliano could provide political input without strongly influencing the decision-making process is nonsense and ignores the obvious reality that the expression of an opinion to a subordinate official by the Prime Minister's Chief of Staff or the Minister amounts to an order. Mr. Pelletier's actions in meeting with Mr. Guité in the absence of Mr. Quail or his representative constituted political encroachment into the administrative domain. It was a dangerous precedent that should not be condoned.

There were two major flaws in the Sponsorship Program, of which an experienced politician or public administrator should have been aware. First, having the program administered by private sector communication agencies was an open invitation to unscrupulous persons to reap unjustified or exaggerated profits; and second, initiating a program of this kind without first developing rules, guidelines and criteria, and without ensuring effective bureaucratic oversight, left the door open to error, abuse and careless administration. Mr. Goodale saw these flaws immediately and froze the program. When it recommenced a few months later, Mr. Goodale discontinued the use of communication agencies in favour of administration by public servants equipped with the proper tools and resources, including newly established guidelines. These elementary measures should have been applied from the beginning.

There is no evidence that Mr. Pelletier was in any way involved in Mr. Corriveau's kickback scheme, although it would have been more prudent for him to investigate the general suspicions that he says he communicated to the Prime Minister when, according to his testimony, he had a hunch that there was something not quite right about Mr. Corriveau. The absence of any evidence of direct involvement in Mr. Corriveau's wrongdoing entitles both Mr. Pelletier and Mr. Chrétien to be exonerated from blame for Mr. Corriveau's misconduct.

But they are to be blamed for omissions. Since Mr. Chrétien chose to run the Program from his own office, and to have his own exempt staff take charge of its direction, he is accountable for the defective manner in which the Sponsorship Program and initiatives were implemented. Mr. Pelletier failed to take the most elementary precautions against mismanagement – and Mr. Chrétien was responsible for him. They should have done in 1996 what Mr. Goodale did in 2002. They should also have done precisely what Ms. Bourgon counselled the Prime Minister to do, which was to postpone making decisions about sponsorship initiatives until a formal process had been adopted for evaluating them. It would have been more prudent for Mr. Chrétien to have accepted her suggestion that responsibility for the administration of the Program be transferred to the PCO or to a Minister, instead of being retained within the PMO. He chose to disregard this advice and, since he is directly responsible for errors committed by Mr. Pelletier, he must share the blame for the mismanagement that ensued.

The Responsibility of Mr. Gagliano

Mr. Gagliano chose to perpetuate the irregular manner of directing the Sponsorship Program that had been adopted by Mr. Pelletier, and, with him, met with and gave directions in person to Mr. Guité, excluding Mr. Quail from the direction and supervision of the activities of a public servant within his department. When he became involved in the direction of the Program, Mr. Gagliano, like Mr. Pelletier, failed to give sufficient attention to the adoption of guidelines and criteria, and failed to provide oversight to what Mr. Guité and his successor, Pierre Tremblay, were doing, all the while systematically bypassing the Deputy Minister, from whom oversight would normally be forthcoming. Contrary to his testimony to the effect that his participation was limited to providing political input and making recommendations about events and projects to be sponsored, Mr. Gagliano became directly involved in decisions to provide funding to events and projects for partisan purposes, having little to do with considerations of national unity.

Finally, just as Mr. Chrétien must accept responsibility for the actions of his exempt staff such as Mr. Pelletier, Mr. Gagliano must accept responsibility for the actions and decisions of his exempt staff, including Pierre Tremblay, who served as his Executive Assistant, and Jean-Marc Bard.

The Responsibility of Other Ministers

On the evidence there is no basis for attributing blame or responsibility to any other Minister of the Chrétien Cabinet, since they, like all members of Parliament, were not informed of the initiatives being authorized by Mr. Pelletier and their funding from the Unity Reserve. Mr. Martin, whose role as Finance Minister did not involve him in the supervision of spending by the PMO or PWGSC, is entitled, like other Ministers in the Quebec caucus, to be exonerated from any blame for carelessness or misconduct.

The Responsibility of the Deputy Minister of PWGSC

Ranald Quail knew that Mr. Guité was meeting with the PMO and later with Mr. Gagliano and that, in those meetings, decisions were being made about the administration of a program for which he, as Deputy Minister, was responsible. He abdicated his responsibility to control, direct and oversee the actions of officials in his department.

There were many reasons to have paid particular attention to Mr. Guité and his organization. First, it was imprudent for him not to know details of what was being discussed at Mr. Guité's meetings with Mr. Pelletier and Mr. Gagliano. If Mr. Quail did not take steps to inform himself of what was going on, he must accept the consequences of irregularities that occurred.

Second, Mr. Guité had a well-known reputation as a public servant oriented to obtaining results by cutting through red tape. This should have alerted Mr. Quail to the possibility that he was not administering the Sponsorship Program according to Treasury Board rules and policies. The nature of the Sponsorship Program, with discretionary spending for political objectives, was such that guidelines and criteria were of particular importance.

Third, the telephone call from Mr. Bilodeau about Mr. Stobbe should have aroused suspicions that if someone in the PMO did not want Mr. Stobbe to follow Mr. Guité's activities, there was something about the activities that needed investigation.

Fourth, the report of the Ernst & Young audit included an unambiguous reference to significant non-compliance with Treasury Board policies. The follow-up was slow and resulted in no changes whatsoever except to confer additional responsibilities to Mr. Guité as Director of the newly formed CCSB.

These combined factors should have provoked a reaction. The duty of Mr. Quail was to better inform himself of the situation and to call Mr. Guité to account for his deficient administration. In fairness to Mr. Quail, he was, in 1996 and 1997, very busy with the enormous problems associated with program review. In addition, he was reluctant to interfere in the Sponsorship Program, which was a priority of the Prime Minister.

The Responsibility of the Liberal Party of Canada (Quebec)

The method of financing the Quebec wing of the Liberal Party of Canada, using kickbacks obtained by Jacques Corriveau from persons deriving benefits from the Sponsorship Program such as Jean Brault (and probably others), is described in the Fact Finding Report. The persons who accepted contributions in cash and other improper benefits have brought dishonour upon themselves and the political party. Michel Béliveau, Marc-Yvan Côté, Benoît Corbeil, and Joseph Morselli deserve to be blamed for their misconduct. They disregarded the relevant laws governing donations to political parties.

The LPCQ as an institution cannot escape responsibility for the misconduct of its officers and representatives. Two successive Executive Directors were directly involved in illegal campaign financing, and